Relationship Road Map
30-Day Challenge

WATERBROOK

Relationship Road Map 30-Day Challenge

A Plan for Every Step of Your Relationship Journey

Stephen Chandler

A WaterBrook Trade Paperback Original

Copyright © 2025 by Stephen Chandler

Some material is adapted from *Relationship Road Map* by Stephen Chandler, copyright © 2025 by Stephen Chandler, published in the United States by WaterBrook, an imprint of Random House, a division of Penguin Random House LLC, in 2025.

Library of Congress Cataloging-in-Publication Data
Names: Chandler, Stephen, author.
Title: Relationship road map 30-day challenge: a plan for every step of your relationship journey / Stephen Chandler.
Description: First edition. | Colorado Springs: WaterBrook, [2024] | Includes bibliographical references.
Identifiers: LCCN 2024034810 | ISBN 9780593194317 (trade paperback) | ISBN 9780593194324 (ebook)
Subjects: LCSH: Single people—Religious life. | Single people— Prayers and devotions. | Dating (Social customs)—Religious aspects— Christianity. | Marriage—Religious aspects—Christianity.
Classification: LCC BV4596.S5 C435 2024 | DDC 248.8/4—dc23/eng/20241114
LC record available at https://lccn.loc.gov/2024034810

Printed in the United States of America on acid-free paper

waterbrookmultnomah.com

1st Printing

First Edition

Book design by Susan Turner

Most WaterBrook books are available at special quantity discounts for bulk purchase for premiums, fundraising, and corporate and educational needs by organizations, churches, and businesses. Special books or book excerpts also can be created to fit specific needs. For details, contact specialmarketscms@penguinrandomhouse.com.

CONTENTS

INTRODUCTION

IF YOU'RE SINGLE AND WANT TO BE MARRIED, THIS THIRTY-day challenge is designed for you.

Maybe you've been out there working the dating apps and you're exhausted by the last seven disappointing dates you've had. Or maybe you're at home right now on your couch and you haven't left your apartment in thirteen days. I know that finding the person God has for you can be hard. I get it. But I also know that there are things you can do to prepare yourself to meet the person you'll share life and ministry with. And that's why I created this thirty-day challenge for you.

Now, if you wanna keep repeating those same bad dates over and over—and never know why you can't change the pattern—be my guest. Or if you want to stay on the couch bingeing Netflix, that's a choice you can make. But if you want to prepare your heart, your body, your mind, and your spirit to meet Mr. or Mrs. Right, then this challenge is for you.

Wherever you find yourself right now, these next thirty days are going to bring clarity, hope, and vision. God knows what your future looks like, and I'm confident that He will guide your steps. Your job is to keep moving forward.

Each day I'll introduce you to an essential component of this journey and offer a challenge—an exercise, an assignment, a practice, a way to reflect—that will help you take your next step. If you embrace the challenge every day, you'll see the fruit in your life. You'll be better equipped for this journey toward marriage. And if you find yourself wanting to *skip* a certain day after you read the challenge, I want you to notice that and gather the courage to *push through* on that day. It might just be your most important step.

This challenge is a gentle nudge, or maybe an aggressive shove, from a friend who really loves you. It's an encouragement to position yourself—or reposition yourself—physically, emotionally, and spiritually to discover the person God has for you. The Bible says that the man who finds a wife "finds what is good,"[1] and I'll add that the woman who finds a husband finds what is good. What you're after is *good,* but you're going to have to be willing to do things differently. I know that doing new things can be scary, but to find something you've never seen before, you're going to have to go somewhere you've never been before.

On this journey, I'm encouraging you to keep your

eyes on the prize. And in this case, the prize is a vibrant marriage in which you and your spouse love and serve each other while influencing the kingdom as only you can. I hope that you can see yourself in a joy-filled, God-honoring marriage one day. But that destination is unlikely without intentionality, prayer, and wisdom. And that's what I am hoping you'll invest in this thirty-day adventure.

Sometimes we get so fixated on the destination that we miss the joy that God is revealing to us along the journey. There's no guarantee that you will be married at the end of this thirty-day challenge. As a matter of fact, I really hope that you're not—that would be a very quick engagement!—but you are laying the train tracks that will lead to happily ever after.

I was friends with my wife for two years before we started dating. Honestly, while she was incredibly attractive and godly, because our friend circle was so tight-knit, it took time for me to realize everything I was looking for was right next to me. When we did start dating, it didn't take long. Ten years, three kids, two dogs, and one wild adventure later, I can testify that everything can change in a moment and God really does have more for you than you would ever dare to ask.

The goal of this thirty-day challenge isn't for you be engaged next month. (Please don't be.) Rather, the aim is for you to develop a plan to pursue dating with the goal of marriage in mind. It's meant to help you be intentional and approach dating in a way that will lead to your good and the good of your neighbor. It's meant to equip you to date in a way that glorifies God.

For thirty days, let's lean all the way in. You will learn so much about yourself and how God made you if you'll commit to the journey. I implore you to fight those two natural temptations—feeling pressured to make something happen or doing nothing—and enjoy the journey! One of the most attractive features of any individual is joy. It's infectious. So, let's make sure that this journey is marked with joy that is rooted in your confidence in God. With Him, you are more than enough, and He has promised to work out this area of your life for your good. As a matter of fact, when it's all said and done, He will work it out better than you would have ever dared to ask for.

So, here we go; let's get started.

Relationship Road Map
30-Day Challenge

DAY 1

Begin with Your Destination
in Mind

OLIVIA AND TWO OF HER GIRLFRIENDS WERE EN-
joying brunch one Saturday morning when the
conversation turned to marriage. Olivia was
single, and her two friends were both married. Over the
course of the conversation, one woman complained *con-
tinuously* about how much time her husband spent playing golf each weekend with his friends and how this had
become a source of much conflict. It sounded like she
harped on her husband about it *every day*. The rift between them had become so deep that they might go days
without speaking to each other.

Olivia's other married friend also shared a bit about
her marriage. She explained how her husband's boss had
taken credit for great work her husband had done. Noticing how upset he was, she stopped what she was doing to

pray with him about the frustrating situation. She even shared how grateful her husband was for the TLC.

As Olivia drove home from brunch, she continued to think about the two relationships and what she did and didn't want in the marriage she hoped to have one day. She began to picture the future she aspired to reach.

I'll bet you know what it's like to prepare for a trip. When you take time off work, pack up the car, gas it up near home, and then hit the road at five o'clock in the morning to meet up with a friend for vacation, you know where you're headed. (If you don't? Well, that's a whole other conversation . . .) And when you're on this dating journey—whether you're still packing the car or you've been driving so long that you're running out of gas—you need to travel *with your destination in mind*. Specifically, I'm inviting you to notice the experience of other travelers who've been there.

I don't know what kinds of marriages you've seen, but God's plan isn't just for you to find someone to make babies with and then grow old and die. The writer of Song of Songs gushed, "I found the one my heart loves. I held him and would not let him go" (3:4). God's good intention is that marriage would be amazing. Joy filled. God glorifying. That's the beautiful destination.

In Jesus's ministry, the crowds who were curious about Him *traveled* with Him. And as He taught them about what it meant to be His disciple and follow Him, He wanted to make sure they had enough "gas in the tank," so to speak. He wanted them to consider—at the front end—what it would take to *finish well*. He offered,

"Suppose one of you wants to build a tower. Won't you first sit down and estimate the cost to see if you have enough money to complete it?"[1] Today is your opportunity to consider where you're headed and if you've got what it takes to make it there.

—————————— **Day 1 Challenge** ——————————

Spend time considering the destination: the marriage you want to experience one day.

List five things about marriage that you're looking forward to:

1.
2.
3.
4.
5.

List five things about marriage that may concern you:

1.
2.
3.
4.
5.

All right, now I want you to get a little more specific. (And because you'll be naming names, remember that this challenge is private. It's between you and the Lord, so *speak freely.*)

When I look around at marriages I've seen over the years, I admire the relationship that _____ and _____ share.

I'd like to emulate their marriage with my own future spouse in these specific ways:

When I look around at marriages I do *not* want to duplicate, a marriage that concerns me is the one between _____ and _____.

I want to be careful not to imitate what I've seen in their marriage for these reasons:

God, show me what You desire
in a strong, healthy marriage.

DAY 2

Check Your Engine

WHEN DEION WAS YOUNG, HIS MOTHER WAS ADdicted to alcohol and drugs. At the age of six, Deion and his twin brother were removed from her care and placed in the foster system. Growing up, they rotated through different homes. At sixteen, Deion was adopted by the foster parents he'd lived with for four years. He didn't date in high school, but when he went to college, he met Marissa during orientation, and they started dating exclusively the first week of school.

Everything was going well in their relationship at first, but after a few months, Marissa noticed that Deion would get angry with her for the smallest things. He would get heated when she was out with friends at night and didn't answer his texts. Or if she went home for the weekend to be with her family, he would act really cold and distant when she returned to school. Eventually, Marissa decided that she couldn't deal with his hot-and-cold moods, and she broke up with him. During his years in undergrad Deion dated two more girls, and both of those relationships had the same outcome.

Before you set off on a long trip, you want to know that your engine is running well. You need to know it's not going to overheat! And if you've been taking care of your car, you likely have that confidence. Deion's social worker knew he would benefit from therapy, but his adoptive parents never made it happen. Throughout his difficult childhood, Deion hadn't been offered the opportunity to care for his engine.

Not everyone's story is as difficult or complicated as Deion's, but we all have trauma—past hurts that have hindered our personal growth and continue to affect our relationships. One of the ways today that you can check your engine is to pause and consider the dating relationships from your past. That's what I'm inviting you to do. And if you haven't dated, or haven't dated much, ask God to show you how *your* old hurts have affected other close relationships in your life. (But, to be clear, a relationship with a committed partner is where old hurts will really interfere. Now you know.) And I want you to hear that this engine check isn't *my idea.* The psalmist announced this about the Master Mechanic: "He heals the brokenhearted and binds up their wounds" (147:3). Heart healing is what God does. However, if we want God to heal our hurts, we need to acknowledge them. Take a moment to respond to the following statements.

- From what I know of myself, the hurts—little and big—from my past that might interfere with my journey include . . .

- From what I know of myself, the inner hurts that God has *already* healed include . . .

One of the ways our old hurts can interfere with our lives today is through the power of fear. Fear is a natural response to being hurt. If we've been wounded, we're *afraid* that we'll be hurt again. It's natural. But it's also something God wants to redeem.

How has the fear of being hurt again affected your relationships with others?

Even though our past hurts can negatively influence our current relationships, like they did for Deion, we can also reap the healing *benefits* of prior relationships. Maybe a previous boyfriend or girlfriend who accepted you entirely helped you believe you are worth loving. Or maybe their appreciation of one of your quirky habits allowed you to love it. Or they may have shared with you their wholehearted love of God's Word. Take some time to consider the following questions.

- What are some of the healthy parts of your previous relationships that you want to repeat in future relationships? Be specific.

- If you haven't been in a relationship, what quality do you value most in your *friendships* that you hope to experience in marriage?

Psalm 147, the one that says God heals the brokenhearted, is a song that celebrates all the good things God does. (If you want to see examples of His goodness, read all of Psalm 147!) Friend, God heals our broken hearts and binds our wounds so that we can love Him, love other people, and love ourselves the way He loves us.

──────── **Day 2 Challenge** ────────

Get serious about offering your old hurts to God.
This week, consider doing one of these four things:

1. Read Psalm 147 and make a list of how God acts toward the brokenhearted.
2. Commit to journaling about the hurts from your past that continue to affect you.
3. Find someone older and wiser who knows your story,

and explore with them how old hurts might still be
bossing you around.

4. Make an appointment with a therapist to explore how
    old hurts might be influencing your relationships today.

> Two broken people can't make a whole
> marriage. When you enter into marriage,
> you've got to be whole in yourself. You
> have to decide to say, "I'm going to let
> God rebuild me. I'm going to let God re-
> store me. I'm going to let Him remake me.
> I'm going to let Him bring back what the
> Enemy stole."

God, speak to me about the hurts
I'm carrying in my heart
and how You want to heal me.

Check Your Engine (Part 2)

FROM THE OUTSIDE, IT LOOKED LIKE KIARI HAD an idyllic childhood. And in many ways, she did. She had parents who loved God, loved each other, and loved their two daughters. They lived next door to Kiari's maternal grandparents, and her grandfather pastored the church the family attended. Kiari had lots of friends and did well in school. She had everything she needed physically, socially, emotionally, and spiritually. Anyone who knew her would say that she was thriving.

Kiari's sister, five years younger, was born with a number of intellectual and physical disabilities. And because Kiari's parents wanted to make sure *Kiari* wasn't neglected, they asked the grandparents if Kiari could stay with them. For the first two years of her sister's life, while her parents were occupied with her sister's visits to nearby doctors and distant hospitals and her physical and occupational therapy appointments, Kiari lived with her grandparents so that she could receive everything she needed.

And while their intentions were good, Kiari's parents couldn't have anticipated the way those childhood years spent living with her grandparents would shape Kiari's heart. Although she *had* friends, she wasn't convinced that they wouldn't drop her if someone better came along. And although she had a boyfriend in high school, she was always waiting for him to leave her. She kept a smile on her face, but the Enemy continued to hiss that she wasn't worth loving.

I'm asking you to check your engine as you embark on this dating journey. For some people, like Deion, the dashboard lights are announcing—insistently—that the engine needs to be checked. But for someone like Kiari, who *appears* to be flourishing, what's happening under the hood is not as obvious.

Get serious about assessing the condition of your vehicle now. We've all had some wear and tear. Sometimes, as in Deion's life, there's been a wreck, and the damage is obvious. But for someone like Kiari, who has felt neglected, diagnosing the problem may not be as clear.

As you're checking your engine today, I also want you to consider *why* you're dating. Is it because you're lonely? Looking for a good time? Or are you dating to honor God as you search for the person He has for you? I don't want you looking to the world for cues about why and how you should date. That's a wreck just waiting to happen. The whole reason I wrote *Relationship Road Map* and this thirty-day challenge is because I'm convinced that you were made for so much more. As you begin, I want you to be clear about *why* you're embarking on this journey.

Today, consider what you reflected on yesterday and ask God, *How healthy am I?*

Because there's not always a blinking light on the dashboard, I encourage you to prayerfully review your life's journey. Year by year, ask God to show you what experience or rupture may have had a lingering effect on your heart. Ask God to open your eyes to something that might not be obvious. Maybe your parents lost track of you at the mall one day. Maybe a kid in the neighborhood bullied you and you never told anyone. Or maybe your parent was emotionally unavailable. Acknowledging these hurts is the first step to healing. Take a moment to record one or two hurtful experiences from the eras of your life listed below.

• When I was a toddler . . .

• When I was in pre-K . . .

• When I was in elementary school . . .

• When I was in middle school . . .

• When I was in high school . . .

• When I was in college . . .

• When I was in my early twenties . . .

• When I was in my late twenties . . .

• When I was in my early thirties . . .

• When I was in my late thirties . . .

You get the idea.

When the prophet Jeremiah addressed the people of

Israel, they'd been beaten up and broken down. And through the prophet, God promised, "I will restore you to health and heal your wounds" (30:17).

Today, I'm inviting you to consider whether your engine is ready for the journey, and I also want you to be able to name *why* you're embracing this adventure.

──────────── **Day 3 Challenge** ────────────

Spend time reflecting on why you're launching into—or recalibrating—this dating journey. Then ask God to show you one experience that has had a lasting impact on your heart, and consider processing that one thing as you did yesterday: in your journal, with a wise guide, or with a professional.

God, I am offering You the hurts inside my heart. Speak, Lord, for Your servant is listening.

DAY 4

Get a Tune-Up

"WHERE ARE YOU?!?!?! AND WHY AREN'T YOU AN-swering my texts?!?!?"

Shawna's anxiety had been building over the course of the evening. Although she was out with her friends, she'd been texting her boyfriend, who was playing basketball with his friends. Her earlier texts began innocently enough: "Hey, boo, just thinking about you." But when he didn't reply, she started imagining the worst. *Maybe he's not playing basketball at all. . . . Maybe he's out with another woman. . . . Maybe he got hit by a car. . . .* And nothing Shawna's girls said could convince her to put away her phone and just enjoy being with them.

Shawna and her boyfriend had been dating exclusively for about three months. And to be clear, he'd given her *no reason* to doubt his faithfulness. But something inside her just started churning when they weren't together, causing her to think the worst. And Shawna could admit that she'd experienced something similar in her friendships over the years. No matter who the friend was, part of Shawna was always waiting to be cut loose or replaced by someone else. And, unfortunately, her anxiety actually drove away people who genuinely loved and cared for her.

We all have these tender parts of our hearts. Maybe a father's absence means that we're not as secure as we could be. Or perhaps we were hurt in a previous dating relationship and we carried that experience into the next. In Shawna's case, her parents adopted a child almost Shawna's exact age when Shawna was three. And she'd always felt jealous of the attention her parents gave to her adopted sibling. We don't always know what issues we're dragging into dating.

What we do know is that the mess we're carrying from the past interferes with our new relationships. When God brought His people out of bondage in Egypt—a land that had been plagued by disease—and brought them into a new land, He promised, "I will not bring on you any of the diseases I brought on the Egyptians, for I am the LORD, who heals you."[1] As you begin, or continue, this dating journey, allow God access to your tender parts, your hurting areas; offer them to Him for healing. I promise that whatever work you do now will benefit you both now and in the future God has for you.

——————————— **Day 4 Challenge** ———————————

Reflect on advice you've received from the older, wiser guides in your life. These people in our lives don't just help "fix" us when we're broken; they also can give us savvy counsel along the way.

List the five best pieces of advice—related to relationships and emotional health—that you have received thus far:

1.
2.
3.
4.
5.

Now pause to consider what's at stake.

What's the *risk* if you choose to ignore your emotional wounds? What is the benefit of acknowledging those core wounds? And what's the *benefit,* or the blessing, of being healed?

God, guide me to the resources I need to be made well.

DAY 5

Hit the Road, Women

IT WAS FRIDAY NIGHT AND THIRTY-SIX-YEAR-OLD Tanya did what she did most Friday nights: She went out to the clubs with her girlfriends from work. Most weekends, every one of the women ended up drinking more than she intended and went home alone at the end of the night. (Though sometimes one would meet a guy and go home with him.) Hooking up wasn't Tanya's style. She might strike up a conversation with a guy and exchange numbers, but her Christian faith was important to her, and she wasn't sleeping around with strangers.

Tanya's twin sister, Tammy, was also single and also wanted to be married one day. Tanya threw some shade Tammy's way and gave her a hard time for spending her weekends at home, reading and sewing. "How are you ever going to meet anyone if you never put yourself out there?" Tanya demanded.

I wanna jump in and suggest that I do think Tanya makes a fair point. But when it comes to being in a position to meet a good man, neither of these sisters is doing the work to show up where the good men are! Now, I'm not saying you won't ever find a solid brother at the club, but it's a lot more likely that you're going to meet a good man if you're more intentional about being in the spaces where he is.

In the Old Testament, we find the story of a widow who couldn't pay her family's debts.[1] After a creditor threatened to take her sons as slaves to settle the debt, the widow begged God to help her. When God's prophet Elisha showed up on the scene, he asked what she had to work with, and all she had was a little bit of oil. In the ancient world, oil was used for everything, so it had value. Elisha instructed the woman to borrow empty jars from her neighbors and pour the little bit of oil she had into the borrowed jars. When she did, every jar was filled! She was able to sell the jars of oil to pay off the family debt and even live on what was left.

Sis, God is in the business of filling up jars. Some examples of modern-day jars you could put out for God to use to help you on your path toward marriage include:

- Dating apps (the serious ones, not the hookup apps) are one jar.

- Co-ed small groups at church are another jar.

- Getting to the gym and being around other people is another jar.

- Signing up for a continuing ed writing class at the local college is another jar.

- Volunteering at a local nonprofit is another jar.

You get it. I want you to be putting out jars in places where God can fill them.

Make a list of all the jars you have available right now. Where are you currently able to meet men? Are you being purposeful to maximize those opportunities? Are there jars—or opportunities!—you can add? Maybe ones you've not considered before?

Maybe you visit a popular brunch space. Maybe you get onto the dating app your girlfriend assured you is not horrible. Maybe you introduce yourself to someone at the grocery store! Be creative about putting out those jars for God to fill.

---------------- **Day 5 Challenge** ----------------

Be intentional about setting out a jar once a week for the next four weeks. If you can't decide which jar or where to put it, I suggest you hop on one dating app that you know has been a win for a friend who is about your age and lives near you (#PutYourselfOutThere).

God, give me courage to put myself out there, and guide me as I do.

DAY 6

Hit the Road, Men

WHEN TY WAS IN A SERIOUS RELATIONSHIP DURing college, his friends didn't love—or even *like*—the woman he was dating. They gave him a hard time when she'd call to check in *constantly*. They cringed when she told him what to wear when he went out. They ribbed him when she told him what time he needed to be back at the dorm. But for three years, Ty limped along in a relationship that just wasn't healthy. When the couple finally broke up, Ty was crushed. He knew that she hadn't been good for him, but he'd chosen to stay in the relationship because he didn't want to be alone.

Today, *ten years later,* Ty is still single. He continues to live at home with his parents and hasn't been on one date since exiting that painful, toxic relationship. He *says* that he'd like to be married, but his actions communicate something else.

If Ty were *my friend,* I promise you that he would have heard from me about his situation. If you're grown and God has not called you to singleness, I want you to be about the business of finding your "good thing." If you're not in that business, I'm going to have some questions for you.

You and I both know that not everyone is going to be up in your dating business. But for this challenge, I want you to give a trusted friend permission to be! The Bible describes a kind of friendship in which we make each other better and stronger. And Proverbs promises, "As iron sharpens iron, so one person sharpens another" (27:17). I want you to choose someone to weigh in on your dating journey who knows you well and wants the best for you. Whether you're holed up like Ty or you're out there on the dating apps talking to Christian girls, you might just assume your friends are cheering you on. But . . . they may not be. The mentors and guides who know you may see something else at work in the way you're going about—or not going about—finding someone. And because we all have blind spots, it's important that you invite these ones who love you to *speak freely* about what they see.

——————— **Day 6 Challenge** ———————

I want you to begin this challenge by taking inventory of where you think you are in the dating journey.

- Am I being proactive in getting to know women and asking them out?

- Am I dating too many women and not being intentional?

- Am I going about it in the right way, in the right places?

- Am I being clear with women about my intentions?

- Should anything concern me about my dating habits?

Then ask a trusted friend or mentor where they think you are in the dating process, offering them the same questions.

- Do you think I'm being proactive in getting to know women and asking them out?

- Do you think I'm dating too many women and not being intentional?

- Do you think I'm going about it in the right way, in the right places?

- Do you think I'm being clear with women about my intentions?

- Do you see anything that concerns you about my dating habits?

I want you to record the conversation so that you can listen to it again and reflect on what they share!

God, please grant me the wisdom to make necessary adjustments and remain purposeful in my approach to dating.

DAY 7

Hit the Road, Men (Part 2)

ARE YOU READY TO BREAK OUT OF YOUR COMFORT zone?

Daniel's grandparents met when they were fourteen years old, and they are now sixty years into a strong, healthy marriage. They still go on dates and get giggly on Valentine's Day. Daniel's parents met as college students and married the weekend they graduated. His older brother met his wife when they were both bagging groceries over summer break during their college years. They just had their second child. No one had to get set up by friends. No one had to go speed dating. They certainly didn't use dating apps. And they didn't even need to gather their courage to visit the singles group of a nearby church. For the happiest couples Daniel knew, it *just happened*.

And while I obviously recognize the ease and benefits of it "just happening," that's not everyone's story. And if Daniel is serious about pursuing a wife, he likely will need to be intentional about making that happen. Remember how the Bible says that "he who finds a wife finds what is good"?[1] Well, it doesn't tell us whether that means meeting someone by chance at work on summer break or putting energy and effort into being intentional (like I hope you're learning to do here). Being intentional begins by looking at how you got where you are.

Today, I'm inviting you to really look at how you've been traveling this road toward marriage until now.

- **Notice:** Begin by journaling what your dating (or "not dating") journey has looked like until now.

- **Evaluate:** Think about whether it's been fruitful or fruitless. Why do you think you've had the results you've seen so far?

- **Consider:** What have you done in the past that you'd like to do differently now?

- **Identify:** Identify someone whom you are interested in getting to know better. (There don't have to be fireworks just yet; the bar is low: Who would you like to know better?)

I want to challenge you to make your interest *known* to another. Don't overthink it. Maybe you just text someone from the singles group at church to ask if they're coming out on Friday night. Maybe you ask your cousin for her friend's phone number and drum up an excuse to meet for lunch one day. Maybe you offer to give someone who's "just a friend" a ride to church Sunday morning.

If you find yourself really resisting today's challenge, I want you to notice that and consider why. Spend some time reflecting on what's holding you back from expressing your interest. See what you can learn, about *you,* by noticing that resistance.

Perhaps you should even stop and jot down your responses to these two questions:

1. What is holding you back from intentionally pursuing marriage?

2. What are your greatest fears about this journey?

Acknowledging your greatest fears is the first step to disarming them.

And listen, I'm not trying to get you to make a commitment to find the person you are going to marry within a certain time frame. I just want to challenge you to put yourself out there and *express interest* in someone you are curious about. Low bar. And whether it goes somewhere or no-where, it's a great exercise for you to learn and grow from.

Whether there is or isn't someone on your radar at the moment, you've still got homework: Come up with three possible ways you can express interest in an individual, now or in the future.

1.

2.

3.

Day 7 Challenge

Express your interest in someone

Q: Pastor Stephen, what if there's truly nobody on the horizon right now? What if I'm really not interested in anyone?
A: Well, if you're all alone in Antarctica, you get a pass. For now.

God, let's do this. Open my eyes to someone worth knowing better.

DAY 8

Avoid These Obstacles

IF YOU'VE BEEN ON THIS JOURNEY *FOR A MINUTE* or have traveled with friends on this road, I don't have to tell you that there are roadside hazards you'll want to avoid. So go on and make up your mind *now* that you'll steer clear of these four dangers.

1. Don't Be Too Picky

You know about "the list," right? It's a checklist of everything you want to find in a mate. Friend, if you cling to a thirty-point checklist of who your future spouse needs to be—and they have to check every box—you're going to be alone for a good long while.

2. Don't Over-Spiritualize This Thing

Ladies, if a guy asks you to grab a cup of coffee, *please* don't tell him that he is moving too fast and pray for four weeks before giving him an answer. If you're curious about the guy, just go drink some coffee! Guys, you don't need wait for God to send you a sign—like a bright star over her Honda in the church parking lot—to ask her out. Definitely seek the Lord's wisdom, but know that you don't need a sign from on high to take that first step and simply show interest. Slow your roll and just get to know someone.

3. Don't Fool Yourself into Thinking You Can Change Someone

When we're getting to know someone, especially some-one who checks many of our boxes, we can be tempted to overlook a few things. If a person is particularly fine, we'll turn a blind eye to the fact that she's never once been on time to meet up. Or we'll ignore the fact that he can't pay his rent even though he's still out there playing the scratchies every day. Hear this: You can't change someone. Be willing to see clearly.

4. Don't Believe That Love Is a Feeling

You know that ooey-gooey feeling you get inside when you see him or think about her? Well, as nice as that is, it's not *love*. Don't get me wrong; it's a great feeling. But it's *not* what should guide your decision-making. While it's important to notice your feelings and what they're telling you, we know that "the heart is deceitful above all things,"[1] and our hearts are, naturally, sinful.[2] That means you can have all kinds of feels for someone who might have no idea how to love like Jesus loves. So, I want you to be careful not to be bullied by your feelings. Or hormones.

Okay, now you know the hazards.

I want us to pause at that first one: "the list."

First, we're going to get real creative and brainstormy, and I'm going to ask you to make that list—a list of things you look for in someone you would consider marrying. This is just for you, so feel free to be honest. Make it as long as you want. Take all the time you need.

•

•

•

•

-

-

-

-

-

-

-

Okay, while you know I don't want you dragging around a long, unrealistic list, I think that the honest exercise of naming all the things you're looking for is really important. But now we're going to do the hard work. I want you to invite God's Spirit to guide you. Ask God to help you consider how you might edit the list to make room for Him to move. Trust God and strive to be open-handed.

First, I want you to look at your list and cross out three things that really might not matter all that much. I did give you permission to dream big in the brainstorming process, and now it's time to weed out a few of the things that may not be *critical* to find in a mate (#DontBeSoPicky).

Then, I want you to return to that list and circle the three things that matter *most* to you. What are the three most important things you can narrow the list down to?

1.

2.

3.

--- **Day 8 Challenge** ---

Share your long list and your short list with two trusted people, and invite their honest feedback.

Our culture has told you that love is an emotion. Society, Hollywood, and your bestie have convinced you that love is about how you *feel*. And if you just find the right person, you can fall in love and live happily ever after.

The problem is that the assignment to "find the right person" sets us up to believe that there's a perfect person.

There's not.

God, You know my heart. Give me a desire for what matters most to You.

Trust the Guardrails

JENNA WAS RIDING IN THE PASSENGER SEAT OF her mom's fancy new Mini Cooper. And as her mom was driving, an indicator kept flashing on the dashboard. "Honey, open the glove compartment and look in the manual to find out what this is." Jenna grabbed the manual for her mom's new car and found the symbol her mom was seeing: an automobile that was angled in a driving lane.

"Uh, Mom," Jenna answered carefully, trying not to giggle, "it says it's a Lane Departure Warning. It means you're swerving out of your lane." After they both laughed about it, the value of the indicator became clear! It is meant to help the driver stay safe by staying in their lane.

There are some guardrails that can help us stay safe when dating by avoiding those who just aren't for us.

They're meant to help you assess who the other person is, identify what they're bringing to the table, and keep you working on being the best you. Here they are . . .

Guardrail #1: Only Date Someone Who Has Demonstrated They Have a Real Relationship with God

Sis, it's possible that this man has checked the Christian box on that dating app but doesn't have a real relationship with God. And if he's really chiseled, you might be tempted to look past that. Brother, she might say she's a Christian, but if the way she's living her life is causing those warning lights to go off inside you, pay attention to them. When you're dating, you need to see evidence that someone is walking with God.

Guardrail #2: Find Someone Whose Strengths Complement Yours

Some of the most beautiful marriages I've seen are between a man and a woman who bring different gifts into the relationship. Maybe he's analytical and she's relational. Maybe she's great with money and he's got an eye for design. While there will likely be ways in which your strengths overlap, I'm encouraging you to find someone whose strengths *complement* yours.

Guardrail #3: To Find the Right Person, Be the Right Person

I've seen single folks get hyperfocused on finding "the right one." But while they're on that mystical quest, they haven't taken the time to *become* the right person. There is a lot of value in using your time and energy as a single person to become who God made you to be. If you aren't investing in your own spiritual health, you're not going to be ready to be a healthy partner.

Day 9 Challenge

Evaluate your current guardrails or determine future ones.

1. What are some practical ways that you can invest in your personal growth? What do you need to do to *become* the right person? How can these investments prepare you for a relationship? For marriage?

2. If you haven't considered guardrails before, which ones would be important to you?

3. If you're in a relationship now, evaluate your guard-rails. Are they working? If they're not, what needs to change?

4. If you're not in a relationship right now, how can guardrails help you effectively navigate your future relationships?

*God, show me how to be wise
and safe on this journey.*

DAY 10

Follow the Rules of the Road

HAVE YOU EVER BEEN DRIVING DOWN A ONE-WAY street and seen another car driving toward you? It's terrifying. Maybe it was dark or the driver was new to town and accidentally turned into the wrong lane of traffic. Maybe it was actually a twelve-year-old unlicensed driver who had no idea what they were doing. Maybe the person had imbibed a bit too much alcohol and wasn't making the best decisions. Or maybe they were just enraged and choosing to drive like a maniac to blow off some steam. When we see them coming in our direction, we just know that it's *dangerous*. And I'm going to suggest that there are some rules of the road, for dating, that are meant to keep us safe on the journey.

Let me break 'em down real quick.

1. Exercise Good Boundaries with People You're Not Dating

If you're not dating someone, don't behave as if you are. (This goes for your body, your time, your money, and your energy.)

2. Exercise Good Boundaries with the Person You're Dating

Yes, I want you to keep healthy boundaries when it comes to sex. But I also want you to be smart about not rushing into emotional intimacy too quickly. Settle down; let it happen when the time is right. Beware of trauma bonding—while you want to look for someone you can be vulnerable with, be careful not to share all your past hurts until you know you can trust the person you are dating. I'm not suggesting you withhold your thoughts and experiences. Just be wise, and know that oversharing can create a false sense of intimacy.

3. Avoid Sexual Sin for Your Sake

Friend, sexual purity is good for you. It protects your body. It protects your mind. It protects your heart. It protects your spirit and your relationship with God. It. Is. Good. For. You.

4. Avoid Sexual Sin So That You Can Be Clearheaded About the Person You're Dating

Being sexually intimate with someone makes it difficult to see clearly. You'll overlook something in the other person that you should pay attention to.

5. Avoid Sexual Sin for the Sake of Your Eventual Marriage

Whether or not you marry the person you're dating, you invest in your eventual marriage—and theirs!—by re-serving sex for marriage. (When you have sex with the person you're dating, you are training your body to think there are options outside of marriage to get your wants and needs met. Think it through . . .)

6. If You've Not Repented of Sexual Sin, Don't Get Married

Failing to repent of all sexual sin—sex before marriage, pornography, adultery, and more—puts your marriage at risk. Don't get married until you've repented of the sins from your past. You do that by confessing your sin before God, asking for forgiveness, and committing to avoid that sin. James's letter to the church also encourages believers, "Confess your sins to each other and pray for each other so that you may be healed" (5:16). That's solid wisdom right there. If this is a practice you've never embraced, I encourage you to confide in a trusted spiritual mentor. *It's powerful.*

- Which two of the six road rules were the most obvious to you? Which ones made immediate sense? Why?

- Which two of the six road rules were harder for you to accept? Which ones did you want to disagree with or reject? Why?

    Okay, for today's challenge, I want you to get serious about owning some practical rules for yourself.

- Do your friends have boundaries in their relationships that you can learn from and adapt for your own relationships (current or future)?

- Write down four boundaries you can put in place with people you're not dating that will help you prepare for dating.

- Write down four boundaries you can put in place with the person you *are* dating (whether you're in a relationship now or hope to be in the future).

---------------- **Day 10 Challenge** ----------------

Commit to implementing the boundaries you chose, now and in the future.

God, give me wisdom to establish healthy boundaries and commit to keeping them.

Follow the Rules of the Road (Part 2)

LET'S SAY YOU'RE TAKING A ROAD TRIP. IF YOU live on the East Coast, we'll say you're traveling to Los Angeles to dip your feet in the Pacific Ocean. And if you live on the West Coast, we'll say you're traveling to Virginia Beach to do the same. Either way, you've got a long journey ahead. (And if you find yourself reading this book twenty miles north of Belle Fourche, South Dakota, the geographic center of the United States, you get to choose which beach!)

As you set off on this adventure, you're envisioning your destination. You can almost feel the soft sand beneath your feet and the waves lapping against your ankles. And you don't want to take any unnecessary risks on the journey that would keep you from your destination.

That means you're going to need to follow the rules of the road: Stay in your lane, obey the speed limit, merge safely, keep your eyes on the road, and stop at red lights. Do those things and you're likely to make it to your destination safely. You understand, intuitively, that safe driving is the way to get there.

When God created a people for Himself, He gave them the Ten Commandments in Exodus 20:2–17. For God's people to flourish, for them to remain safe and healthy, they were instructed to follow God's "rules of the road." And when we name and practice some healthy boundaries around our relationships, we can also flourish and thrive.

We agreed yesterday that when your destination is *marriage,* there are rules of the road to follow if you want to arrive safely. Most of the road rules I suggested yesterday were healthy boundaries around sex. And today I want to name others that also contribute to a happy and healthy marriage.

- Seek the Lord daily.

- Work on your own mental and emotional health.

- Welcome counsel, as you date, from married Christians further along in their walk with God.

- Develop personal spiritual disciplines.

- Commit your relationship to prayer: alone, with friends, and with mentors.

- Pursue financial stability.

- If you are dating, review your boundaries around sexual purity with your partner.

Yesterday, I asked you to identify four *personal* boundaries around God's gift of sex that you can put in place with people you're not dating to prepare for dating. I also asked you to identify four boundaries you can establish with people you *are* dating. (So, to be clear, that's "just friends" boundaries and "more than friends" boundaries.) And today we considered other rules of the road that help us thrive—as individuals or in a relationship.

Now I want you to refer back to Day 1 of this thirty-day challenge. Specifically, notice what you wanted, what you were looking forward to, in *marriage*. To jog your memory, review Day 1 and then note your answers here:

1.

2.

3.

4.

5.

Today I want you to consider how the road rules we're discussing—both the boundaries you identified yesterday and also the types of guidelines I mentioned today—can help you to achieve what you said you wanted on Day 1. Spend a bit of time reflecting on that connection. How will the boundaries you chose yesterday protect you? How will they affect your experience when you arrive at your destination? In light of your goals on Day 1, are there any boundaries you need to add?

——————— **Day 11 Challenge** ———————

Identify individuals who can hold you accountable on your way to your destination—to follow the rules of the road you've established. Text or call one of them today!

When you choose to follow God's plan *before* marriage, you're actually making an investment in your eventual marriage.

God, help me travel safely to reach the destination You have for me.

DAY 12

Watch Your Speed

WHEN YOU'RE DRIVING, DEPENDING ON WHETHER you have a short fuse or a long one, you might find yourself getting irritated with other drivers on the road. (Or is it just me?) First, you've got the daredevils on crack—those drivers on the freeway who are weaving in and out of lanes while traveling about ninety miles an hour. *They're terrifying.* Then you've got the ones who are really comfortable creeping along in the far-left lane. These clueless drivers, happy and slow as clams, are likely going about twenty miles below the speed limit. They're in no hurry, and they don't have a care in the world! And then you might be at an intersection, maybe at a red light, and you've got someone who's distracted by their phone. Long after the light turns green, everyone behind them is just . . . stuck. Drivers who aren't moving with the speed of traffic can be maddening.

Well, I see the same thing with couples who are dating. (I don't get quite as agitated by them as I do the drivers because . . . it's *their* business. But I do *care* about these couples.)

There are the couples who are planning how many kids they want to have together on their second date! That's too fast. Then there are the ones who've been dating for six years and they're just not making it to the altar. In most cases, that's way too slow. And then there are those who are just *stuck*. This couple might be trying to check all the boxes—finishing their education, getting jobs that pay well, or accomplishing any other random goal—before they wed. They're stuck.

You already know I really believe that if you're grown and you've done the work to get healthy (in all the ways), you should be driving at a reasonably safe speed toward marriage. So, for today's challenge, I want you to consider what a good timeline is for you to reach the destination (#EatingWeddingCake).

- If you are *single,* consider a good timeline for you. When do you want to make your next move? When would you like to be married?

- If you are *dating,* identify where you are on the timeline. Are you moving toward marriage? Why or why not?

—————————— **Day 12 Challenge** ——————————

Acknowledging that there's a lot out of your control (help 'em, Jesus), suggest a reasonable time by which you'd like to be married: _____.

Then I want you to share your answer with an older person who cares about you and invite their input. Ask, "Is there anything you know that I need to do if I want to meet this goal? Speak freely." (That's bold, right? Be brave. Really give this person who loves you the freedom to speak into what they see in your life.) This is big, friend. You have so much to gain from today's challenge!

God, because all of my days are in Your hands, I commit the timeline of my marriage to Your care.

DAY 13

Heed the Warning Signs

LET'S SAY YOUR BEST FRIEND HAS BEEN DATING someone for about three months. They've brought this person around you and other friends, *as they should*. And you've noticed what you think is either a yellow or a red flag.

The first time your friend brought this person by to meet you, you smelled alcohol on their breath. It was nine o'clock on a Saturday morning. *Okay,* you reasoned calmly, *maybe it's some kind of new mouthwash I'm not familiar with*. But when your BFF brought this person to the wedding of a mutual friend, their date got really drunk. And really loud. And really obnoxious. *Okay,* you thought, *it's a party. People drink at celebrations*. But when you had this couple over to dinner at your house to get to know the person better, your bestie's significant other showed up drunk.

The first warning sign? We'll call that a yellow flag. It signaled that caution should be exercised. But the third one? That flag was redder than a stop sign.★

The psalmist asked of God, "Open my eyes that I may see" (119:18). When Paul prayed for the believers in Ephesians, he offered, "I pray that the eyes of your heart may be enlightened" (1:18). Friend, *this is what God does.* And it's a great prayer to pray: "God, open my eyes to see what You see."

Whether you're the person who's dating or you care about the person who's dating, you want to pay attention for any warning flags. Maybe the person still lives at home with their parents because they've never been able to hold down a steady job. Exercise caution. Maybe this person has a package from Amazon Prime on their doorstep *every single day* because they have a problem with shopping and spending more than they make. Exercise caution. Or perhaps this person talks incessantly about their ex. Exercise caution. When you or others are dating, you want to keep your eyes wide open to notice everything that matters.

--------------------- **Day 13 Challenge** ---------------------

While it can be easier to spot the cautionary flags in others' relationships, I want you to pause to really look at your own life—past and present.

★ Discover more about yellow flags and red flags in *Relationship Road Map.*

- How have you spotted red flags in your previous relationships? Who did you weed out because you recognized warning signs?

- On the flip side, what flags did you *choose to ignore* in previous relationships that you should have paid more attention to? Why did you ignore them?

- If you are in a relationship now, are there any yellow or red flags? (This is just for you, so write freely. Don't try to filter your answer. Write down any big waving red flags, and also write down any teeny tiny wonderings or concerns.)

If you're seeing flags that are warning you about a relationship you're in now, find a friend you trust and ask their opinion.

**God, open my eyes so that
I can see what You see.**

DAY 14

Heed the Warning Signs
(Part 2)

OKAY, I MENTIONED THAT IT CAN BE EASIER TO spot cautionary flags in others' relationships than in our own. Am I right? (FYI, that's a rhetorical question.) I want you to warm up for the Day 14 challenge by creating a master list of cautionary flags. I'm giving you the gift of considering *other people's relationships* and asking you to create a list of yellow flags and red flags.

Yesterday I said that "God, open my eyes to see what You see" is a great prayer. Another prayer that God loves to answer is "Give me wisdom." James said, "If any of you lacks wisdom, you should ask God, who gives generously to all without finding fault, and it will be given to you" (1:5). As you look for yellow and red flags, ask God for wisdom.

To make sure you're really being thorough and com-

prehensive, I'm going to prime the pump to suggest actual relationships—real or fictional—that you can use as
source material. So, as you're brainstorming yellow and
red flags, I'm suggesting that you consider:

- Your parents' relationship

- Your grandparents' relationships (if you don't know
  about their relationships, now would be a good time
  to ask them)

- Your siblings' relationships

- Your close friends' relationships

- Your not-as-close friends' relationships

- Relationships you've seen on film or television, real or
  fictional

- Relationships that you've read about in books, real or
  fictional

And as you're considering these couples, ask yourself, *What signals should I look for that indicate caution is
advisable?*

Okay, go big or go home.

List as many yellow flags as you can:

•   •

•   •

•   •

•   •

List as many red flags as you can:

•   •

•   •

•   •

•   •

If you gave that exercise 100 percent, great job.

Now it's about to *get real*. You know all those flags you recognized in others' relationships? Well, now I want you to run through that list and ask yourself, *Would a potential partner recognize any of these qualities in me? Am I throwing up any yellow or red flags?* Go back through the lists you made and circle any concerns that could potentially be true of you.

Friend, this may feel like hard work. So, I want you to hear that it's *really important* work. Maybe there's a flag that you've noticed in yourself before and haven't taken the time to work on. Or maybe God will open your eyes to something that you haven't wanted to see in yourself. While it can feel uncomfortable, it's vital to notice what should *rightly* give someone pause about marrying you. Invite God to open the eyes of your heart and mind. Then, listen . . .

Day 14 Challenge

Having done the vulnerable work of looking for yellow and red flags in your own life, identify what you can do to rectify the areas of your life—your personality, your habits, your flaws, and more—where there could be yellow or red flags.

God, give me the courage to see clearly, and give me the wisdom to make changes.

DAY 15

Travel with Others

TIM AND SAVANNAH WERE BOTH STUDYING abroad in Portugal for the second semester of their junior year of college. Tim attended a college in Chicago, not far from where he'd grown up, and Savannah attended a school near her family's home in New York. Tim and Savannah met during the program's orientation in mid-January. In fact, they stayed up all night after the first day of orientation talking about their shared love of '70s R & B, their passion for anime, and how they each had siblings who were identical twins. Their relationship got serious pretty quickly.

Because they were both so excited about the relationship, they eagerly shared details about each other with their parents. But the day-to-day experience of getting to know each other and dating was largely done in isolation. In Portugal, Savannah had a roommate who spoke German and some English, but her roommate was often busy with her own friends. And while Tim had a roommate, they weren't really friends. Because they'd paired up so quickly, neither Tim nor Savannah built a friend group after arriving in Portugal. Most of their days and nights were spent with each other.

You can probably begin to imagine the dangers of dating in isolation. Tim and Savannah's isolation happened on another continent, but I'll bet you've known couples—surrounded by nearby friends and loved ones—who made choices that separated them from community. Maybe they insisted on spending all their time with each other and neglected their own friendships. Maybe they simply weren't interested in introducing their new boo to family and friends. There are countless ways that dating in isolation can happen.

You were made for *more*. In the New Testament, we can see that followers of Jesus formed a community of people who loved God and loved one another. Beloved, you were never meant to date in isolation. So I'm asking you to open your heart to begin to imagine what it looks like to travel this season of your life within a community of Christians who know you and love you.

Pause to spend some time creating a list of dangers that Tim and Savannah's relationship might face because they are dating in isolation.

-
-
-
-
-

The antidote for dating in isolation is, of course, inviting others into your relationship. That could mean that you invite your significant other to hang out with your friend group. Or you might bring the person you're dating to your church one Sunday to introduce them to folks there. Or, when the time is right, you might find a not-weird way to introduce them to your family members.

Today's challenge has two parts. I'm inviting you to commit to dating within the context of community.

---------------------- **Day 15 Challenge** ----------------------

*Start a list of individuals and couples who can share your
journey and get to know the person you date:*

•

•

•

Identify an individual who can walk beside you through
a current relationship or a future one and provide godly
counsel. Also identify a godly and fun couple who have
been successfully doing it God's way whom you can learn
from, whether you're currently single or partnered.

*God, thank You for the godly women and
men who love me and can walk with me
on this journey.*

DAY 16

Rely on Seasoned Travelers

MARIO AND CARMEN BOTH CAME TO KNOW Christ through a campus ministry when they were students at UCLA. They were friends for two years before they started dating at the beginning of their junior year. By the end of that year, the couple was talking about marriage.

Mario had never known his father. He'd grown up with a devoted single mother who raised him and his two brothers on her own while working long hours. Along with her sister, Carmen had grown up in a two-parent home, but her father, an alcoholic, had recently died. So, neither Mario nor Carmen had witnessed a healthy marriage in their childhood homes. In fact, there weren't any examples in their lives of thriving Christian marriages.

A man named Ryan who served as the director of the couple's campus ministry was discipling Mario. Ryan was single and just a few years older than Mario. Ryan knew that neither member of the couple had ever seen marriage done well. So, when Mario and Carmen began discussing marriage, Ryan introduced them to an older couple he knew from church.

Justin and Diane had been married for thirty years and raised three children who all knew and loved Christ. The first time Mario and Carmen played board games and shared dinner at Justin and Diane's home, they ended the evening in prayer. Justin and Diane invited the young couple to continue to share life together, and eighteen months later, Justin walked Carmen down the aisle. In the early years of Mario and Carmen's marriage, the older couple continued to invest in them.

Maybe your experience is similar to Mario's or Carmen's. I know that these days it can be rare to witness healthy marriages that have stood the test of time. I want you to begin to consider who these wise guides might be. In Paul's letter to Titus, his son in the faith, he reminded Titus that the job of older women is to teach younger ones how to grow in godliness (2:3–5), and he exhorted Titus to set an example for the young men by doing what is good (verses 6–7). In the same way, I'm encouraging you to seek out godly couples who can shepherd and guide you. They may be in your church or your neighborhood. They could be the parents or grandparents of a friend. It might be the marriage of a supervisor at work or a professor you've admired. Keep your eyes open for these couples.

Whether you are dating now or not, who are some godly couples you would like to learn from?

-

-

-

-

As you consider these couples, make a list of what qualities their marriages possess that you would like to see in your future marriage:

-

-

•

•

Note: If you really don't have access to a couple like this, talk to an older friend or pastor who might be able to help point you in the right direction.

―――――― **Day 16 Challenge** ――――――

Whether you're dating or not, make contact with a couple from whom you'd like to learn.

When you're dating, you need older spiritual mentors who have your back. Maybe, like me, you have a godly, praying parent. Or it might be your pastor or other older, wiser individuals at your church. There's such a thing as having "holy jealousy" for the life of someone older than you—because you're seeing a life that's submitted to God, and that's what you want. That's who you want on your team.

God, show me and connect me to the older couples I need to know—before I date and while I'm dating.

DAY 17

Pay Attention to Other Drivers

IN THE OLD TESTAMENT, MOSES SENT TWELVE SPIES to scope out the land of Canaan that God was giving to His people.[1] Moses wanted the deets: Who lives there? What's the agriculture like? What else can you find out? And while ten of the spies came back with a negative report, throwing shade on the land they'd seen, two spies—Joshua and Caleb—came back with a good report and the confidence that God would help them and give them the land.

Pastor, I've been tracking with you on this whole thirty-day challenge, but what on earth can this have to do with my dating life?

Trust me.

Before you ever date someone, I want you to spy out the land. You've done great work thus far, but this is the first step in the actual dating process. When you're spying out the land, you're observing someone in their natural habitat. Just like on Animal Planet, you're learning through observation. You're that field observer who's collecting data.

How do they behave when they're around members of the opposite sex?

Is their language salty or sweet?

Do they post half-nude selfies at the gym?

How do they respond when they encounter someone in need?

As you're around someone in a casual setting, you can notice how they behave.

On this dating journey, you're a *spy*. The first step in dating is *not* asking someone out. Or being asked out. The first step in dating is to spy out the land. You're discerning the character of the man or woman whom you may be considering. And I'm convinced that you can determine a lot about a person without ever dating them.

Friend, I knew the type of woman I was looking for, and so I had my eye on my future wife, Zai, before we ever spent time alone together. And one of the things that really impressed me was how she treated her friends when it wasn't easy to love them (my words, not hers).

So, as you do your spy work, here's how you can find clues:

- Observe their social accounts. Learn what you can online.

- Spend time with them in groups.

- Get intel from those who know them well. I want you to ask people who know them whether or not they have good character. Don't invite or entertain gossip, but do listen carefully to how others, particularly their close friends or family members, describe them.

———————— **Day 17 Challenge** ————————

Conduct a secret spy op on yourself!

Remember, this thirty-day challenge is for you, not anyone else. That means that you gain the most from this effort if you are completely honest. Be brave, friend. You're the one who will reap the benefits.

- If someone were spying you out, what would your social media tell them about you?

- If someone were spying you out, what would your behavior in a group tell them?

- If someone were spying you out, what would your friends—if they were being completely honest—tell them?

I've got one more. I'm inviting you to be real imaginative on this one . . .

While I don't anticipate anyone who is spying you out to plant secret cameras in your home—and, to be clear, you should absolutely press charges if they do that—consider what that person would discover if they did see your behavior in private.

- What green flags would they see?

- What yellow flags would they see?

- What red flags would they see?

Day 17 Bonus Challenge

*If you're in a relationship, recall and note what you observed
when you spied the other person out.*

God, open my eyes to see myself clearly.

Pay Attention to Other Drivers
(Part 2)

WHEN THIRTY-YEAR-OLD MICHAEL STARTED WORK-
ing as a junior executive at a company that pro-
duced beauty products for women, he suddenly
got a lot of attention from the single women at his office.
One of them found lots of reasons to stop by his desk and
chat with him. Sometimes it was loosely veiled as a "work"
conversation, and other times not so much. One of them
had a friend who knew Michael's younger sister. And this
co-worker took a special interest in his sister who, like her,
had been on the cheer squad in undergrad. One remem-
bered that he'd mentioned carrot cake, and so she brought
him a slice from a cake she "just so happened" to make over
the weekend. As someone who'd never been swarmed by
women, Michael wasn't mad about what was happening.

When Michael shared about the situation with his
father, his pops gave him some good advice. He coun-

seled Michael to take time to observe these various women who were showing interest in him before rushing into anything. "Do the research," his dad advised. (That's old-school for "spy out the land." Respect.) And Michael took his dad's counsel to heart.

We'll call the first woman Chatty Cathy. As she chattered on, rarely leaving room for him to get a word in, Michael noticed that she shared other people's business, particularly things that would be considered gossip. She talked about folks from the office and even her friends he didn't know. It felt *wrong*.

We'll call the second woman Cheerful Cherrie. When Cherrie shared that she'd used TikTok to make the connection to Michael's sister, he knew she was *also* spying out the land. Okay, I see you, Cherrie. But when Michael did the reverse research, he learned about a few red flags from their mutual acquaintances that concerned him.

We'll call the third woman Carrot Cake Carla. Michael liked what he was seeing. He saw Carla organize meals for a co-worker who was out of work due to surgery. As they chatted, he learned that her relationship with Jesus was the most important thing in her life. And when they joined other co-workers for dinner one evening after work, he noticed that rather than talking about herself all night, she took a genuine interest in others.

Now, when I'm challenging you to spy out the land, I'm not asking you to make it weird. Don't be creepin' around their apartment complex after dark looking for clues. I'm inviting you to use integrity. Checking out someone's socials isn't stalking; after all, socials are out in public for anyone to see. So, notice what they're putting out there in the world. If you're reading someone's profile on a dating site, give 'em a little grace if they misspell a word or are wearing a T-shirt of a pro team you hate. You don't gain anything by judging people too harshly. When John describes the arrival of Jesus in the world, he notes that Jesus came from the Father "full of grace and truth."[1] That's the balance you're after: Seek truth; extend grace.

—— Day 18 Challenge ——

If you're not in a relationship, I want you to be intentional about spying out the land. So, choose one or two people, and get to it. Spy it out.

• What does their social media tell you about them?

• What does their behavior in a group, in the workplace, or in their natural habitat tell you about them? What do you notice about their interactions with others?

• If you have access to their friends—without making it weird or being intrusive—what do their friends say about them?

If you *are* in a relationship, I want you to think back to what kind of data you had access to before you started dating your bae.

• What did you know about this person before you started dating?

• What do you wish you had known before you started dating?

God uses your season of singleness to prepare you for marriage.

God, guide my steps, and give me insight and discernment.

DAY 19

Communicate with Other Drivers

CAN WE TALK ABOUT *TALKING*? BECAUSE PEOPLE mean different things when they say "talking," and I want to make my meaning plain.

When Andrew's brother asks him about a girl he's mentioned a few times, the twenty-year-old frat boy tells his brother, "Yeah, Sylvia and I are just *talking*." And because bro is not new to this, he suspects that while they haven't made a commitment to each other, Andrew and Sylvia are absolutely hooking up.

To be clear: That's not what I mean when I suggest you should begin talking after spying out the land. I am not suggesting that you hook up.

I'm suggesting that you should conduct communication that is written, spoken, and in person while in groups with other people. Talking is how you continue to learn more about someone after you've spied out the land.

Paul's prayer in Philippians was that the believers would "be able to discern what is best" (1:10). And that's what you're asking God for in the talking phase: *discernment*.

Let's say you met someone on a dating app. Their profile signaled that they check some of your boxes and seem like a good person. To get to know them better, you start *talking*. In this scenario, here's a loose progression of how a relationship might unfold:

- **Messaging on a dating app:** With the safety of not giving out your personal information too quickly, you have a conversation with someone you've met *on the app*. You begin to learn about who this person is. (And because you know that any ol' catfish can say any ol' thing on an app, you're not getting too deeply invested in this person until you have a way to verify that what they say truly matches who they are.)

- **Texting:** You can learn enough about someone from messaging on an app—like their full name so you can search for and find them online—that you feel comfortable sharing your phone number. (If you want to be extra careful, you can always use a free Google Voice number instead of your own personal cell.) So you can scrap the app and continue to learn about someone by texting them.

- **Talking on the phone:** Have you seen the movie *Nobody's Fool*? For a variety of reasons, the main character was talking to a man she had met online for a year without speaking to him on the phone (#RedFlag). Let me say that texting was not enough for Danica to discern who this guy was. It wasn't until they were finally able to connect "voice-to-voice" that she was able to discover a bit more about him. When you begin speaking on the phone, you have the opportunity to learn a lot more about someone.

- **Video chatting:** Video chats—made popular for dating during Covid—are a great way to spend time with someone and learn more about them. You hear their voice, get a glimpse of them and their space, and discover more about who they are.

- **Doing stuff with groups:** Nothing is a substitute for being with someone in person. So be creative about how to invite this person you're getting to know into your world. Invite them to brunch with you and your friends. Welcome them to join a meetup at a jazz-in-the-park event over the weekend. Eventually, have them come to game night at your friend's place. You not only get the benefit of in-person contact, but you also have the valuable opportunity to see them interact with others.

Did you notice what kind of interactions did *not* make the approved list? Setting up your first interaction as a hike in a remote wooded location was not on the list. Meeting up at a hotel in a strange city? Not on the list. Going inside to see his favorite artwork that's hanging in his apartment? Not approved. For all kinds of reasons, be

smart about the talking phase of getting to know someone.

Get creative with the questions you ask in order to
learn about who someone is. Remember, you don't need
to go too deep too fast. Here are a few ideas I hope will
inspire you to come up with your own questions.

- When you were a kid, what did you want to be when
  you grew up?

- What do you admire most about each of your parents?

- What would your best friend say are your strengths and
  weaknesses?

- If you had a wall of heroes, who would be on it?

- Is there a cause or issue about which you're really pas-
  sionate?

- What do you admire or appreciate about your closest
  friends?

- What's something you're really proud of?

- Is there something, a quality in yourself, that you're
  working on right now?

Here are some questions for you to help you begin to
think about this phase of dating:

- n your experience, what have been the telling signs, or dead giveaways, that you've discovered about someone's character while *talking* that you might not have picked up on while messaging on an app or texting?

- How can you be creative and intentional about your next talking phase? How can you make it interesting?

Day 19 Challenge

Write a list of questions you'd like to ask someone you are talking to. Consider running this list by a trusted Christian friend or mentor for feedback before you begin asking questions.

God, as I'm getting to know someone,
teach me to see what You see and
hear what You hear.

DAY 20

Use Your Signals

FRIEND, AS YOU'VE BEEN MOVING THROUGH THIS thirty-day challenge, you've been doing good work. I hope you've been willing to take an honest look at yourself and others. That's foundational, and it's a great investment into whatever comes next. And now . . . *drumroll, please* . . . we're going to dig into actual dating.

This. Is. The. Fun. Part.

When you decide to make the move from talking to someone to dating, it gets good! And the very first phase of dating *should be fun*. Even though you're still paying attention to what you're learning, I want you to enjoy this time. In fact, if you are not having fun, that's probably a sign that whoever you are dating isn't the person for you.

To help you begin thinking about fun ways to get to

know someone, I want you to clear out some space on your hard drive by brain dumping some popular first date options that are just tired and overdone and un-original. I'll get you started, and then you keep going . . .

1. Have a picnic in a park.

2. Get dinner at Chili's.

3.

4.

5.

6.

7.

8.

9.

10.

I'm going to give you ten first date ideas, and I want you to come up with twenty more. I'm pushing you on this because when you do the work to come up with twenty fresh ideas, you're going to think of much more interesting activities than going out to coffee or grabbing dinner.

1. Go roller-skating.

2. Have fun bowling.

3. Take a cooking class.

4. Volunteer together.

5. Visit the zoo.

6. See a play at the theater.

7. Go out to a jazz club.

8. Explore a museum.

9. Zip around the city on rented bikes or scooters.

10. Attend a basketball game.

   Now, dream up twenty more creative first-date activities:

11.

12.

13.

14.

15.

16.

17.

18.

19.

20.

21.

22.

23.

24.

25.

26.

27.

28.

29.

30.

———————————— **Day 20 Challenge** ————————————

Identify one of the ideas on your list that you have never heard of someone doing on a first date, and then either test it out with the person you are dating or keep it in your back pocket for your next first date!

Creator God, You have all of the ideas, so help me to imagine a date that would delight You and the person I'm with!

DAY 21

Choose a Co-Pilot

EVERY ENGAGEMENT STORY IS UNIQUE.

Yeah, a lot of them include a ring hidden in some dish at a fancy restaurant or an idyllic nature setting with family and friends secretly hiding in the bushes and filming the whole thing. But for every couple, that moment when they get engaged is one they'll always cherish. (Except for the horrific ones you can watch on YouTube. A few people will try to forget theirs.)

Today, on Day 21, we're going to talk about the engagement phase of dating, and whether you are single, dating, or engaged, I think you'll find something here for you.

When I begged Zai to help me plan my birthday party while we were dating, she thought it was super weird to make such a big deal of *twenty-six*. But that's because she didn't yet know that it would actually be an *engagement* party. With everyone watching, I got down on one knee—in front of Zai's mom and sister—and proposed. In fact, knowing that she loved poetry, I actually read Zai the first and only poem she would receive from me for the next decade. (Yeah, I totally tricked her into marrying me.)

On the twenty-first day of the challenge, I want you to hear two things, loud and clear:

1. If you're dating and it's time, I want you to handle your business. Get engaged. Okay, that was easy. Done. Check that box. (JK. I know it's not quite that simple. But to make it plain: *Men,* handle your business. *Propose* already. And if he's not doing it, if he's tarrying, women, you can "encourage" him to do it.)

2. Whether you're dating or not, I want you to be able to envision what the engagement period is for.

Today's challenge is to *handle your business.*

—————— Day 21 Challenge ——————

Today, I want you to take some time to consider what might be holding you back from making progress on your journey toward marriage. No matter where you find yourself, I have a challenge for you:

- For the men who are dating seriously: If you've been dating for a while, ask yourself if it's time to take the leap. If not, what's stopping you? Are there any areas in your relationship that need to be realigned with God's intentions?

- For the women who are dating seriously: If you've been dating for a while, ask yourself what could be preventing him from taking the plunge. Are there any areas in your relationship that need to be realigned with God's intentions?

- For the men or women who are not dating someone seriously: Notice how you are naturally wired when it comes to dating. Are you more likely to tarry and take your time, or are you more likely to jump the gun to jumping the broom? Reflect on *why* you might function this way.

Okay, the hard part of the Day 21 challenge is over. Now you can breathe. But I actually do want to pause and encourage you to *do engagement right*.

A lot of people expect the engagement period to be a nightmare hazing for the couple—a bridezilla season of choosing flowers, sampling cake flavors, picking wildly priced gowns, and pulling your hair out while trying to create a seating chart where no one is near their ex. The couple thinks, *This is how it's supposed to be. If we can make it through this, then we can weather being married to each other.*

Let me go ahead and stop you right there. Engagement is a time for you to plan and build what is to come. The flowers and the cake and the clothing and the seating chart have to get done, but they have *nothing* to do with building a solid marriage. You know what does contribute to the kind of marriage you want to have? What matters most is you and your partner having conversations about what matters most. You're developing a unified vision for faith, family, finances, the future, and healthy life rhythms. (Yeah, the alliteration fell apart there at the end.)★ The apostle Paul exhorted believers, "Encourage one another and build each other up."[1] During your engagement, I want you to be thinking about how you can be responsible for yourself, and also build your partner up, in each of these five areas.

Wherever you are on your dating journey, jot down any thoughts you have *today* about what you hope to experience in marriage:

1. **Faith:** How will your faith—as an individual, as a couple, as a family—be lived out?

2. **Family:** Consider if, when, and how you hope to grow your family, how you'll raise kids together, and how you'll one day care for your larger family (such as aging parents).

★ You can learn about this in a bit more detail in my book *Relationship Road Map*!

3. **Finances:** Ask how you'll deal with any existing debt, who will be working outside and inside the home, and how you will save and spend and give together.

4. **Future:** What do you hope to see in your future? Will it include homeownership, and if so, how will you plan for that? Where do you hope to live? How will you navigate, together, the unexpected?

5. **Healthy life rhythms:** How will you use time well, pursue physical and emotional health, and navigate friendships during marriage? Will you encourage your spouse to go to counseling? Make an agreement that if things get difficult in your marriage, you'll go to counseling together.

God, quicken my heart to know both when to enter into engagement and how to do it well.

Kick a Hitchhiker to the Curb

NOT LONG AFTER MANNY AND MARIA STARTED dating, they began to imagine, separately, the possibility of building a life together. Manny was a barber, and Maria could imagine him cutting their kids' hair in the kitchen. Maria was a chef, and Manny dreamed of the holiday meals she'd serve when they gathered with their extended family.

When Maria found out that Manny enjoyed drinking fine whiskeys, she didn't quite know how to think about it. She'd never seen him *drunk,* but no one in her family drank anything stronger than wine. She decided to pay attention and learn more. When Maria found out that Manny smoked cigars, she didn't quite know how to think about that either. She wasn't thrilled about it, but she could see how much Manny loved the cigar club he visited on Thursday nights. About a month or two into dating, Maria noticed a big stack of lottery tickets in Manny's car. He explained that it wasn't a big deal, but she could see that he'd spent thirty dollars on each one.

A few months into their relationship, when Maria suggested how Manny could write off some work expenses on his taxes, it came out that Manny didn't pay taxes. He divulged that he'd actually been hauled off in handcuffs from his barbershop six months earlier, but he assured her it was all under control. He hadn't paid the back taxes, but he wasn't concerned.

Maria continued to think and pray on what she was learning about Manny. She knew he struggled to pay some of his bills, but she also saw him spend hundreds of dollars a week, sometimes *in a day,* on cigars and alcohol and lottery tickets. A few weeks later, she tried to ask Manny some questions to understand more about the taxes, and he exploded in rage. She'd never seen him even get annoyed before, but there seemed to be a tender spot inside him, and this really triggered him. Maria was able to keep her composure during the conversation, but then she didn't hear from Manny for a week. He wanted to keep dating, but when he refused to talk about money with Maria, she ended the relationship. And she never once second-guessed her decision.

Both the Old and New Testaments of the Bible caution us to be discerning about who we spend time with: "A companion of fools suffers harm."[1] "Bad company corrupts good character."[2] "Do not be yoked together with unbelievers."[3] God helped Maria discern that—for a variety of reasons—she and Manny could not be *yoked*

together. I'm inviting you to ask God for wisdom about
if and when you should end a relationship.

─────── Day 22 Challenge ───────

*Consider previous relationships, and ask yourself if there
were any signs that you should have ended things sooner.
Why or why not? Also reflect on times when ending the
relationship turned out to be the right decision and why.*

If you're in a relationship today, ask yourself if you are in the
right relationship. Is your faith aligned? Are your values aligned?

And if you don't have any experience in relationships,
spend some time considering what your deal-breakers
might be. (And think about how to spot them before the
relationship gets too serious.)

> *God, give me the courage to do the
> hard thing when it's the right thing.*

Wherever you are in your journey—before
you get hitched—you have permission to
call it off. Maybe you look at the person
beside you and you realize, *Oh no, this is
not my co-pilot. This is a hitchhiker, and
they've got to go!* It will take courage to
break it off, but you can do it.

DAY 23

Assess Him as a Traveling Companion

REMEMBER MARIA FROM YESTERDAY? WHEN SHE was considering her relationship with Manny, she didn't quite know how to think about it. Since they'd come from such different backgrounds, she wanted to give him the benefit of the doubt. (*And . . .* she really liked him.) She didn't want to be too "judgmental." As a result, she just wasn't sure *how* to think about what she was seeing.

I've put together a series of questions—just four very manageable ones—that women can ask about the men they're dating to help Maria and others like her. To be clear, you're not posing these questions *to* the person you're dating. You're spending time with God to *consider* them with Him.

I'll make it simple: You're looking for a man of God who is being transformed to look more like Christ. Paul's letter to his boy Timothy exhorted, "You, man of God, flee from all this, and pursue righteousness, godliness, faith, love, endurance and gentleness. Fight the good fight of the faith."[1] That's the kind of man you want to be after.

When Maria reflected on these questions you're going to tackle in today's challenge, they helped her decide how to think about what she was noticing. Specifically, they helped her notice two yellow flags (using alcohol to cope and not making wise financial decisions) and two ginormous red flags (rage and extended periods of emotional withdrawal).

Day 23 Challenge

As I mentioned, I have four questions for you to carefully consider regarding the person you are dating or want to date.

If you're a woman who's dating someone, ask these questions about your boo. (You'll get the most out of this challenge if you're brutally honest and don't hold back.)

If you're a man who's dating, take a stab at answering these *about yourself.* (I promise you, brother, it's a great investment.)

If you're not dating, use the space under each scale to describe the related qualities that you'd like to find in a partner.

Pinpoint your boo—or yourself!—by putting a mark on each arrow as a way to measure where he falls on that spectrum.

1. Is He Sovereign ┼─┼─┼─┼─┼─┼─┼─┼─→ Submitted?

The man who is sovereign over his own life is calling all the shots without consulting God. The man who is submitted is not only seeking the mind of Christ, but he's also obedient to follow His leading. On the scale from sovereign to submitted, mark where you'd place him.

And now offer some evidence for why you scored him as you did. What do you see in him that helped you locate him on this spectrum?

2. Is He a Captain ┼─┼─┼─┼─┼─┼─┼─→ a Crew Hand?

The captain is the one who charts the course. And when the storms come, he protects everyone onboard and steers them to safety. The crew hand? He's looking for the first chance to bail and save himself. On the scale from captain to crew hand, mark where you'd place him.

And now offer some evidence for why you scored him as you did. What do you see in him that helped you locate him on this spectrum?

3. Is He Broke ┼─┼─┼─┼─┼─┼─┼─┼─┼─► Burgeoning?

This question is about dollars, but it's not about being a gold digger. If the man you're considering is low on liquid assets, it could be because he's invested his time, money, and energy into what's coming next, such as training or education. So look at how responsible he is with what he has, and imagine how that will influence his—and maybe your—future. On the scale from broke to burgeoning, mark where you'd place him.

And now offer some evidence for why you scored him as you did. What do you see in him that helped you locate him on this spectrum?

4. Is He Humble ┼─┼─┼─┼─┼─┼─┼─┼─┼─► the Hulk?

The man who is humble is able to pay attention to his emotions and manage them appropriately. The man who's the Hulk has not done his work, and he lacks control of his emotions. On the scale from humble to Hulk, mark where you'd place him.

And now offer some evidence for why you scored him as you did. What do you see in him that helped you locate him on this spectrum?

What do the answers to these four questions tell you about him/yourself? How will you respond?★

God, show me what You desire to see in me and see in them.

★ Women, learn more about these qualities you do, and *don't*, want to discover in a man in *Relationship Road Map*!

Assess Her as a Traveling Companion

ALL RIGHT, ON DAY 24 OF THE CHALLENGE, WE'RE fixin' to turn the tables. Just as there are questions that women need to be asking about the men they're dating, there are questions that men need to be asking about the women they're dating. (And, women, since you read yesterday's challenge, you know how this goes. You'll have the opportunity to do a little self-assessment today. Stick with me, because this is a really valuable investment you can make.)

Guys, I encourage you to spend some time with the last chapter in Proverbs, which describes a "wife of noble character" (31:10). Read it for yourself, but I'll tell you right now: She's a boss! She cares for the poor, brings you good, and makes bank. Truly, check it out.

Guys, when you reflect on these four questions, they can help you assess what you notice in the woman you may be dating. These are the kinds of questions that will shed some light on green, yellow, and red flags.

———— Day 24 Challenge ————

If you're a man who's dating, ask these questions about your boo.★ (You'll get the most out of this challenge if you are brutally honest and don't hold back.)

If you're a woman who's dating, take a stab at answering these *about yourself.* (I promise you, sis, it's a great investment.)

If you're not dating, use the space under each scale to describe the related qualities that you'd like to find in a partner.

Pinpoint your boo—or yourself!—by putting a mark on each arrow as a way to measure where she falls on that spectrum.

1. Is She a Sea Breeze ┼┼┼┼┼┼┼┼┼➤ a Tsunami?

The woman who's a sea breeze can manage her affairs with poise and grace. People want to be around her because she's

---

★ Men, learn more about these qualities you do, and *don't,* want to discover in a woman in *Relationship Road Map!*

refreshing. She's peaceful. But the woman who's a tsunami? She is all about the drama and seems to bring chaos wherever she goes. On the scale from sea breeze to tsunami, mark where you'd place the woman you're dating.

And now offer some evidence for why you scored her as you did. What do you see in her that helped you locate her on this spectrum?

2. Is She a RAV4 ┼┼┼┼┼┼┼┼┼┼➤ a Roller Coaster?

The woman who's a RAV4 is stable. She's reliable. She's dependable. Especially when it comes to expressing her emotions. She's not bullied by them. The woman who's a roller coaster? She's unpredictable. And you might not know, from day to day, which version of her will show up. What about the woman you're dating? On the scale from RAV4 to roller coaster, mark where you'd place her.

And now offer some evidence for why you scored her as you did. What do you see in her that helped you locate her on this spectrum?

3. Is She a Daughter ━━━━━━━━━━▶ Delilah?

*In the Bible, Samson fell for a seductress named Delilah,
and he lost everything as a result. The most important
question for you to ask of the woman you're dating is,
"Does she know that she's a daughter of the King? Or
is she still using what her mama gave her to get where
she needs to go?" On the scale from daughter to Delilah,
mark where you'd place her.*

And now offer some evidence for why you scored her as
you did. What do you see in her that helped you locate
her on this spectrum?

4. Is She Fierce ━━━━━━━━━━▶ Fearful?

*The woman who is fierce has had her needs met by God.
She's secure in Him. On the other hand, the woman who's
fearful is afraid that she'll lose herself in a relationship.
(And if she expects her husband to be her fulfillment,
she might be right!) She's bullied by fear. On the scale
from fierce to fearful, mark where you'd place the woman
you're dating.*

And now offer some evidence for why you scored her as you did. What do you see in her that helped you locate her on this spectrum?

What do the answers to these four questions tell you about her/yourself? Based on what you learned, how will you respond?

*God, show me what You desire to see
in me and see in them.*

DAY 25

Notice the Mileage

EVERYONE WHO KNEW TWENTY-FIVE-YEAR-OLD Ashley thought she was fantastic. And she was. She was active in her church and served as a volunteer in the youth ministry. She was working on her master's in social work. She even mentored a teenage girl through the Big Brothers Big Sisters program. She was just one of those people whose light really shined brightly. And when Curtis spotted her at church one Sunday, he noticed the glow. After inquiring with a few mutual friends, Curtis began finding ways to spend time with Ashley in groups, and then they started dating. Exactly a year after their first official date—ice cream sundaes and axe throwing, if you must know—Curtis proposed to Ashley over another ice cream sundae date.

Their wedding wasn't fancy, but it was a joyful cere-
mony with food and music and flowers and centerpiece
contributions from all their friends. Exhausted, they
drove two hours to the beach where they'd enjoy the first
week of marriage honeymooning together. Well, that
was the plan.

After Curtis dragged all their luggage into the Airbnb,
the newlyweds flopped onto the king-size bed, still fully
clothed. When Curtis turned toward his beloved for a
kiss, Ashley froze. Her heart raced in her chest, and she
felt panicky. Though the couple had stayed pure while
dating, they'd both agreed that they were looking forward to being intimate as spouses. When Ashley explained she was as surprised as Curtis by her reaction, the
pair wrote off her response as fatigue at the end of a long
day. But when the hesitation she noticed the first night
blew up into a full-blown panic that kept them from
being intimate, the couple realized there was something
they needed to work through.

After the honeymoon, when the couple sought help
from a therapist, Ashley revealed that as a girl she'd been
assaulted by a neighbor. She hadn't mentioned it to Curtis, she explained, because she just didn't think of it often
and preferred not to.

I want to suggest that Ashley and Curtis would have
benefited from discussing her childhood experience in
premarital counseling. Not because it would be a deal-
breaker but so that each of them could see what they
were signing on for and be prepared for it. I also under-

stand that a lot of us bury what's painful and that the roadblock may not make itself known until . . . it does. I encourage you to do your best, during engagement, to have some of these hard conversations.

And there are other types of personal information that I want you to share with your partner before you get married:

- What are the person's faith convictions? What do they believe about God, prayer, and Scripture?

- Is this person truly *submitted* to God? Can they hear from God and make changes based on His prompting?

- How will the two of you live out faith together? In what congregation will you worship?

- In relationships, what has been this person's history of consensual sex?

- Has this person endured physical or sexual abuse? If so, how have they addressed the trauma from that experience? Have they been to counseling?

- How does this person manage money? (What did they see in their childhood home? How do they manage money today? Will this person work once you're married? After children? How will your shared finances work?)

- What has this person's experience of marriage been? (What was their parents' marriage like? What good marriages have they witnessed? What bad ones? If they've been married previously, learn as much as you can about that relationship.)

- How does this person anticipate growing a family? (Birth? Adoption? Fostering?)

- How was this person parented? (Were their parents strict? Are they close to their parents? Why or why not? How were they disciplined as a child?)

If you're not yet engaged, I hope you'll hang on to these questions to consider together when you *are* engaged.

For today's challenge, what I want you to do is answer these *about yourself.* It's another great opportunity you're giving God to open your eyes to what you may need to work on as you move toward marriage.

─────── Day 25 Challenge ───────

Make a list of your life experiences that need to be discussed before you get married.

-
-
-
-
-
-
-
-

-

-

God, You have been with me every moment of my life. Open my eyes to see what I need to see.

DAY 26

Read the Instruction Manual

A CLASSIC OLD-SCHOOL ROM-COM FROM THE late eighties is *When Harry Met Sally*. It shows a relationship between a single man and a single woman who—in the beginning—is sort of prickly. At the jump, Harry and Sally are not fond of each other. And over the course of the years, they have an ongoing debate over the timeless question, "Can a man and a woman be 'just friends'?" Sally says they can. Harry says they can't because there will always be sexual tension between them.

What that conversation did *not* include was any discussion of how one's *faith* affects the answer. So, let's take it off the movie screen and say we're in *church*. There's this myth that guys can't have female friends and women can't have guy friends. You're either dating each other or avoiding each other. *You know I'm right.*

As Christians, we can go in these two weird directions. Either we make it super spiritual and avoid contact with the opposite gender altogether (so as to not fall into temptation, maybe?), or we might play at being BFFs—even when the other person is dating someone—and then one person catches feelings.

Then, for fun, let's add one more layer of complexity: Maybe someone is spying out the land, checking you out, and your buddy-buddy friendship with someone of the opposite gender signals to *that spy* that you're not available! (Or, if they find out you are available, it's going to raise all kinds of questions.)

If you're in one of those BFF relationships where you talk on the phone every night and text into the wee hours of the morning, either you're lying or they're lying. Maybe not intentionally, but you are *playing* at dating.

Paul challenged believers in the early church: "Be devoted to one another in love. Honor one another above yourselves."[1] That's your assignment. You honor another person by not keeping an absurd distance; you honor them by getting to know them. And you *also* honor the other person by refusing to *play* at dating.

Day 26 Challenge

Get honest about how you're navigating your relationships with the opposite sex now. As you look at your friendships with people of the opposite sex, are there any ways that a current friendship could be misleading—to you, to your "friend," or to others? What does a close friendship like that communicate to others who might potentially be interested in you?

What do *you* need to do to handle your business? (Hint: Guys, you need to fish or cut bait. Women, please know that you can initiate the conversation and say, "Hey, what's up here?")

God, give me wisdom about the friendships
I have with people of the opposite sex.

DAY 27

Examine the Wiring

IN THE EARLY NINETIES, THERE WAS A POPULAR book called *Men Are from Mars, Women Are from Venus.* The big idea, which the author names in a funny way, is that men and women are fundamentally *different.*

And today I want to give you an opportunity to explore that big idea before I offer my two cents. I think this is a really important question, and I think that the way you answer it is absolutely going to influence how you experience marriage: In what ways has God created men and women to be fundamentally different?

I hope you looked inside and put on the page all the thoughts you have about how men and women have been uniquely designed. And now I'll share my thoughts.

God designed man for the responsibility of providing for and protecting his family. God designed man to function as a priest, as Jesus did, introducing his family to God. Paul wrote, "The husband is the head of the wife as Christ is the head of the church."[1] Then he becomes the standard-bearer by establishing the family's values. The family's identity. He's the visionary for the family. A family that lacks a man's presence is, in some ways, deficient. Every family needs a man.

Who do you know who best embodies this godly manliness in his family? (Share some names and also offer *evidence* of how they function in this way.)

The woman in the family is, naturally, to be a nurturer. God has wired women to pay attention to the physical and emotional needs of those around them and equipped them to meet many of those needs. I also want to get spiritual here. I think the woman is, in many ways, the prophetic voice in the household. She often sees what appears impossible as being *possible*. The woman is the one to breathe dreams and possibilities and potential into a family. A family that lacks a woman's presence is deficient. I'm thinking of the sensitivity a woman brings to a family. A family needs a feminine presence. Every family needs a woman.

Who do you know who best embodies this godly womanliness in her family? (Share some names and also offer *evidence* of how they function in this way.)

Day 27 Challenge

You've considered how this uniqueness is expressed in others, so now make a list of what natural skills God has gifted you with that will help you fulfill your role in a godly relationship.

-
-

-
-

-
-

-
-

-
-

God, show me how You have created me uniquely feminine or uniquely masculine.

God never designed the government to prepare people for their destiny. God didn't even design the church to launch people into destiny. That's also not the purpose of education. God designed the family to *prepare* people for their destiny.

Examine the Wiring
(Part 2)

I DON'T HAVE TO TELL YOU THIS, BUT TO CLAIM that God made women and men distinctly different is considered countercultural these days. I don't want to get into *all of that,* but I do want to name the fact that I recognize God's design in the Garden of Eden, where man and woman were made for each other, as a *good* design. I think God's genius is evident in how He has created women and men to be different—for the good of one another, for the good of families, and for the good of the world.

And because I know that a lot of people, women *and* men, feel some kind of way about the biblical concept of a wife's submission to her husband, it's really important to me to point out that the order we see in Scripture never diminishes women. In fact, the Bible actually offers this beautiful snapshot of an esteemed woman who is a *boss* in

Proverbs 31. (I happen to be married to one of these Proverbs 31 boss women.)

Don't assume that the Bible has only antiquated things to say about human relationships. Assume it has *true* things to say about human relationships.

─────────── **Day 28 Challenge** ───────────

Notice how you've seen God's good design in action.

- When you consider the roles of men and women in marriage, list the ways you've seen these roles lived out in *successful relationships* around you.

- Did either of your parents, or other loved ones, fulfill their God-given roles in marriage?

- How has that—seeing these roles lived out well, or *not* seeing them—affected the way you understand roles in marriage?

God, show me my unique design
and how You intend for me to
bring it into marriage.

DAY 29

Arrive Safely

IN GENESIS 2, EXPLAINING WHY HE WAS FIXIN' TO create Eve, God announced, "It is not good for the man to be alone" (verse 18). My hope and prayer in this thirty-day challenge is twofold: I want you to see that the destination you're heading toward is *good*. The journey you're on is worth it! And I also want to offer you some practical directions to make it there safely. If you've done the work, you've now got some tools in your toolbox to help you to travel well.

This challenge may be the first time—when it comes to marriage—that you've been given the opportunity to be really intentional about pausing to consider where you've been, to notice where you are now, and to take intentional steps forward to make it to your destination. Tomorrow is the day to step into the future, and today is the day to reflect on where you've been and where you are now. This is why today, Day 29, I want you to spend some time considering where we've been.

• What was particularly *memorable* from this thirty-day challenge? What do you think will stick with you five years from now?

• What from this challenge *surprised* you the most? What was something new that you'd never heard before?

• What from this journey was a literal *challenge* to the way you've always thought about dating or marriage? What is something that you find yourself wanting to resist or push back on?

——————— **Day 29 Challenge** ———————

Identify where you are, today, on this journey toward marriage.

As you look at the arc of the journey outlined in this book—the tune-up to get you ready for the journey, traveling safely, identifying a traveling companion, and eventually making it to your destination—where are you today? Most importantly, what have you learned about *yourself* on this journey?

Here's a pro tip from a mechanic and navigator who's seen more than a few broken down travelers: If you've made it to the dating stage or the engagement stage, that doesn't necessarily mean you don't have work to do; you may have missed an important step in the earlier stages of the journey (#BeforeYouSawThisMap).

So, based on what you've discovered in this challenge, what phase of the journey do you need to revisit? What work do you need to do?

God, guide me as I take my next steps—both stepping back to do any work I missed and also stepping forward into the good future You have planned for me.

DAY 30

You Got This

YOU DID IT! YOU MADE IT THROUGH ALL THIRTY days! Now that you have a clear road map and have identified where you are in the process, it's time to outline your next steps.

--- **Day 30 Challenge** ---

What are three things you can do immediately to prepare yourself for dating?

1.
2.
3.

The point of this thirty-day challenge is to give you very specific things you can do to navigate dating, engagement, and marriage well. So, as we wrap, I want to offer you a few very *practical* rhythms, or practices, that you can begin to knit into your life.

- Spend time daily with the Lord in Scripture and prayer.

- Focus on who you want to be and where you want to go.

- Seek out a mentor who you can start talking with about each step of the journey—from spying out the land to dating to engagement to marriage.

- Serve in the church.

- If you are single and want to be married, put yourself out there—take that first step to meet someone.

If you can't commit to tackling all five of these, I encourage you to choose two or three that you can implement—starting *now*—to help you get on track for dating God's way.

God, You know all of my days. Teach me to trust You as I walk in Your way.

Mile by mile and turn by turn, make good choices that honor God, honor yourself, and honor others. You can do this.

CONCLUSION

THIS IS THE MOMENT WHEN THE FROG TURNS INTO A PRINCE, when the princess wakes up and realizes that you're her knight in shining armor. Or should we go with *Love & Basketball*? This is the moment when Quincy still chooses Monica—even though she lost the basketball game. Okay, I guess I'm just being a hopeless romantic right now. Life may not end up like the movies, but your story is still going to be amazing, and it's just the beginning. Yes, it's the end of this thirty-day challenge, but it's also the beginning of a journey of discovery, exploration, joy, and maybe even some disappointment. Don't get nervous. That's a great thing! That's called life, and there's a whole lot of life ahead of you to live.

My goal is that you would take the challenges of this book and make them a lifestyle. We've all seen the picture of the man who stopped digging right before he struck gold. Don't let that be you. Don't settle for a frog when God has a prince for you. I know sometimes this journey can be depleting and it's easy to get discouraged when we don't find our forever person quickly.

Here are some keys to not giving up on the journey: Value all relationships, not just romantic ones. As you expand the community that you do life with and are intentional about the people who get access to you and the people who don't, you're going to see your world enlarge. And in that enlargement, you are going to run into some eligible candidates. Another key is to make finding a life partner a part of your life, not the obsession of your life. Don't let your desire for or apprehension of marriage consume you. Just like you focus on your health, your career, and your faith, make your romantic life a major part of your life but not the axle of your existence. Please don't forget you are the answer to someone's prayer. In this season, they are also praying for you and looking for you.

What a beautiful journey this will be. This journey will end with an amazing person who's beyond anything you would have ever asked God for. When you get there, a brand-new journey begins. Grab a road map and enjoy the ride!

NOTES

Introduction

1. Proverbs 18:22.

Day 1: Begin with Your Destination in Mind

1. Luke 14:28.

Day 4: Get a Tune-Up

1. Exodus 15:26.

Day 5: Hit the Road, Women

1. See 2 Kings 4:1–7.

Day 7: Hit the Road, Men (Part 2)

1. Proverbs 18:22.

Day 8: Avoid These Obstacles

1. Jeremiah 17:9.
2. See Romans 5:12.

Day 17: Pay Attention to Other Drivers

1. See Numbers 13.

Day 18: Pay Attention to Other Drivers (Part 2)

1. John 1:14.

Day 21: Choose a Co-Pilot

1. 1 Thessalonians 5:11.

Day 22: Kick a Hitchhiker to the Curb

1. Proverbs 13:20.
2. 1 Corinthians 15:33.
3. 2 Corinthians 6:14.

Day 23: Assess Him as a Traveling Companion

1. 1 Timothy 6:11–12.

Day 26: Read the Instruction Manual

1. Romans 12:10.

Day 27: Examine the Wiring

1. Ephesians 5:23.

Practical, Biblical Guidance for Every Step of Your Relationship Journey

The dating scene can feel disorienting and overwhelming—the apps can make you feel like there are too many options while your experience tells you there are none. Despite these challenges, you can learn how to date thoughtfully and intentionally, all while keeping your character and integrity intact.

The practical companion guide to *Relationship Road Map*, offering a plan for every step of your relationship journey—from single to dating to engaged to married.

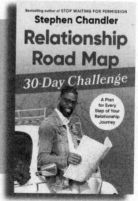

 **WATERBROOK**

Learn more about Stephen Chandler's books at
waterbrookmultnomah.com.

MAXIMIZE YOUR GOD-GIVEN GREATNESS